www.finishinglinepress.com

Going out of Business

poems by

Kelsey Campbell

Finishing Line Press
Georgetown, Kentucky

Going out of Business

ACKNOWLEDGMENTS

To Mom, Dad, and Kristen—You give me courage.

Publisher: Leah Maines
Editor: Christen Kincaid
Cover Art and Design: Mary Ellen Chandler
Author Photo: Louie Tangca

Printed in the USA on acid-free paper.
Order online: www.finishinglinepress.com
            also available on amazon.com

Author inquiries and mail orders:
Finishing Line Press
P. O. Box 1626
Georgetown, Kentucky 40324
U. S. A.

Table of Contents

Withdrawals

Street lights cast phantoms
on my living room floor
as I comb through the navy
shag carpet. Hands shake.
Frantic fingers pick
past fabric strands,
graze the perimeter
by the baseboards.
Then fingers sweep
slowly over the whole
as orange morning pools,
helps me look. I know
I didn't drop a speck.
I check and cautious-creep,
hunt for the glimmer
of a vanished grain.

The Definition of Insanity

I tried to master throwing rocks
when I was young. Slung medium stones
from my great-grandmother's driveway.
They cracked. Shards sputtered off,
flecks of yellow and brown rocks chipped
after each hit. And bounced. I desired
to see amethysts and emeralds in their cores
but each center resembled their outsides;

and I've done the same with poems.
Arm pops, deep shoulder throws
of words to blank, rigid objects,
wanting one to shatter. Slow,
each blow weakening the subject
until it splits, slight, and I use my
thumbs to pry apart the halves.
Inside predictable. Not what I expect.
I pick up another and smash it.
Disappointment shutters down,
rakes along the bones of my spine.
Then I resolve to pick up
and throw another stone.

The Abandoned House

A stone's throw away
from Grandma Mattie's,
and used for storage.
It creaks, heavy with smoky
windows and mahogany mystery.

Rust resides on the shutters
and coon traps litter
the long, cement porch
and block the open door.

A staircase chewed—
and rotten baseboards curl
and lure nature,
like seven-year old girls
who cannot bring their white
tennis shoes inside the threshold

or write about what's shadowed
against the dusk-curtain of dread
which was staked and tented
between her and the front porch steps.

A Basement

the kind only found in old houses—
with narrow stairs and no handrails.
Deep indigo must,
you know the smell:
wet iron or cardboard.
The scent attached
to the word "titanium."
I stack the boxes of my brother's
baseball trophies in the corner.
He gave up on his dreams
right after my niece arrived.
I'm making room in our house
for yellow packages of diapers
and hand-me-down toys.

Big windows line vertically down
half the wall and view into the black
trench built against the window.
Any basement-dweller witnesses
the contents of the gutter's stomach:
a piece of mulch,
some stray leaves,
or the neighbor's cat
which sometimes crawls

through the grate—
his front paws outstretched,
jagged nails protruding.
His back arched, orange
hairs raised on end,
prickly.

The gutter—
with its dingy blocks—
houses any dirty creature
under a foot and a half tall.
See the dirt washed in
through the grate,
or see a domestic cat,
forget having kittens,
instead kill a blue jay for sport
and ignore it in its den.

Down here in the gray must and rust
there's nothing to see
except for the cherry blossom tree,
across the yard
with its frothy red and pink orbs
shooting and sparkling

up from the grate of the gutter—
an overgrown halo over grime.

Snippets

The eyes of scissors rest loose
around her narrow fingers
as she snips photos, articles, fabrics,
and pages from instruction manuals.
Gray hairs and fading health,
she wanes from malnutrition
and years of worry. Her mind
still precise and lengthy
in stories about him, but sliced short
when it comes to what she's done
that day. People avoided, and time lost
among the snippets of paper scattered
on the light-pink comforter,
pilling from age. Most items
remind her of him, especially
pumpkin-oranges, tractors supplies,
photos of mountains, leather
swatches, and ads for cigarettes.
The clutter of moments
have no singular story,
only feelings of the past.
She has to keep him
there, on their bed in front
of her. Every aspect of him
must remain the same, like the scent
of tobacco and the one ebony curl
against his forehead. He'd rest
his tan arm, covered in oil stains,
behind his head as he lay outstretched
on their shared bed watching
her read, her mouth slightly moving,
kissing the words instead of his lips.

Half-Decent

He could learn to love my pinkie finger.
It's slender, and curves, slight, in the right
places. Only two wrinkles crease across it.
Today there are no hangnails. My fingernail stands
tall, far enough off the tip, its head, round.
The enamel, light-pink, girly.

My right ankle is alluring.
It's skinnier than most, bows out,
into the roundness of my calf.
The skin around my foot's bones is tight
and supple. I plucked the one hair
that grows there.

The ellipses in the middle of my curls
aren't half-bad. They hold all the moisture
while the ends fray, jagged-dry, like the fringe
of a nappy rug. The middle curls don't crinkle
like the hairs near my part-line. They're soft,
with cavities for his perfect fingers to hide.

30

Someday my prince won't come
and on that morning I'll be rinsing
off blackberries in my small, pink
kitchen, barefoot, and as skinny
as a needle. In the afternoon
I won't consider hurling myself
off a cliff. I'll call my mother
instead—perhaps twice because
I love her. She'll tell me what
she bought at the farmer's market.
At night I'll watch long wisps
of gray clouds hide, then reveal,
the moon as I put dishes away
in the cabinets. Every day he won't
come, and every day I'll resolve
to stop waiting for him to appear.

He Died on Top of Me

and the full pale-white weight
of him suffocates me as I struggle
to push or roll him off.

And our relationship
is summed up in this:
We're still fully clothed.

I jostle my hips to teeter
him. He's firmly planted—
we are stomach
to stomach, nose
to nose, open eyes
to open eyes.

His pupils are dark and slick
like a crow's wing. Maybe
I've murdered him. His cold
hands are still behind my neck.

My skittish fingers find his stiff ones—
link them like a frayed rope
to an iron anchor—and twist
his wrists to his sides in surrender.

I've never been this forceful
with him and it's a shame
that this is how it ends:
One gave up
and the other still struggles
to breathe.

New Territory on the Road Home

My head rested
on the ridge

of your shoulder.
My arm, a white

river, stretched quiet
ripples across your chest.

A sigh too lumbering,
an arm, vast and desperate

retracts, a phantom moon.

Rain on I-40

Gray cotton swabs of fog
suspended between boundless
clouds. Dreary river roads slithered
over the hips of the mountain range.

I was on the edge of Asheville—
waste-deep in road trip.
Five more hours and an ocean
of water between me and the end
of routine and planned every days.

A shadow void strung off the precipice,
stretched down the mountain's roots
where deer and hunters hide.
I examined the plunge and rounded
the ridge, chasing guardrails.
Tires catch their breath over puddle
pockets, praying not to hydroplane.

Then the sky cracked.
A golden core oozed
out and seeped
north and south.
Yellow and pale
blue ponds blotted
the charcoal horizon.
Its reflection simmered
on the interstate.
A cloudy mirror.

The Body at the Bottom of the Mountain

Unseen guard rails and undisturbed,
overgrown grass border a straight
mountain road with a sharp
left turn. Restricted from the sudden
plunge: gallons of deep-breath
air and green mountains.

It's a way I sometimes took
to go home. Even though
a whisper of wondering
made my eyes flit
toward the drop-off,
I never felt like careening.

Blurry eyes, from drink
or cataracts of depression,
made you shoot off
like a rocket
or dying star,
shimmering
then fizzling.

The waning grasses
waved and rattled
the railing awake.
Yellow reflectors
lit the way down.
Thraking of trees,
the crunch and crash
curbed while mute
pebbles chase after you.

I know you better dead
than if you were alive.
With out-of-state plates
you entered North Carolina
homes through raspy gossip
and late-night news casts.

And guilt hangs like the iron
crane they used to fish
out and haul up your crumpled
car, because for a month
I drove past you eight times
but never saw the signs.

Caryatid

I.

Liquid plaster gurgles
into the mold, gelatin-
whole then hardens cold.
A cast of a stomach and heart
cracks and chips when she pops
it out of the cell. Ruined.

II.

Big gulps of liquid plaster
bubbles down her thin esophagus,
slinks into curves and quiet-
firms, fills a willing stomach.
The body forgets itself.
A fossil, a pedestal

The Myth of the Ferris Wheel in the Woods

Once a goat's head hung
from the limbs of these trees.
Its body missing, its cardboard limbs
ripped down in a thunderstorm.
A carnival was set up in a clearing
of this forest. The dizzy music blurred
colors of the Tilt-awhirl then died
when the kids went missing.
Most ran off to get drunk
on punch behind the pine trees,
then staggered back to find
parents and funnel cakes gone
along with the cardboard chickens
and pigs hanging from the trees.
They noted the lone goat noosed
on a limb. They took it as a sign
and tore it down.

House Scavengers

Three buzzards contemplate suburbia
as they pick at a carcass on the outskirts
of pale houses. Red heads jab, endless.
Dab their white beaks in blood and ponder
homeowners associations and vinyl sidings.
Imagine life by ponds with Canadian geese,
their talons in fresh mulch and thick grass.
But they comb through blonde hair, poke
out two blue eyes, and scar a fresh, round
teenage cheek, and know it'll never happen.

Going out of Business

My mind is a shop
with an ocean-teal door.
Stained-glass mobiles of memories.
hang from the Southern prickles
of a popcorn ceiling. Bouquets
of book pages are stacked
beside Beatles sheet music
and religious tracts from hair creams
on how to cure unruly curls.

My mind is a store
in a town no one visits.
The floors creak from use and the door
is stiff, hard to close and difficult to open.
Strings with red discount tags hang
from the ungodly misshapen forms
on the shelves in the dark corners.
Here, everything is over-priced
but everything is for sale.

Kelsey Campbell grew up in the piedmont of North Carolina, but the mystery of the state's mountains has been a constant inspiration for her writing. A graduate of Asbury University in Kentucky, she received her Bachelor's degree in English and creative writing. Kelsey lives in Virginia where she is a staff writer for a nonprofit. She is currently working on a fiction manuscript as well as a second collection of poetry. This is her first poetry chapbook.

www.ingramcontent.com/pod-product-compliance
Lightning Source LLC
LaVergne TN
LVHW021129080426

835510LV00021B/3368